THE MUNCHIAN O

The Munchian O

MEREDITH WATTISON

PUNCHER & WATTMANN

For Charlie and Maxine

First published in 2020
Published by Puncher and Wattmann
PO Box 279
Waratah NSW 2298
http://www.puncherandwattmann.com
puncherandwattmann@bigpond.com

ISBN 978-1-925780-67-3

A catalogue record for this book is available from the National Library Australia.

Cover design by Miranda Douglas, cover photograph by Meredith Wattison
Typeset by Brenda Thornley and Christine Bruderlin
Text set in Adobe Garamond
Printed by Lightning Source International

Australia Council
for the Arts

Australian Government

This project has been assisted by the Australian Government through the Australia Council, its arts funding and advisory body.

'How to become oneself, how to know the question and the answer of oneself, when one was merely an unfixed something-nothing, blowing about like the winds of heaven, undefined, unstated.'

D.H. Lawrence, *The Rainbow*

'My probing thought often turns towards that original source, towards that reverse nothingness.'

Vladimir Nabokov, *The Gift*

Foreword

This collection brings together uncollected work that Meredith Wattison has written between 1982 and 2017. These poems are unrelated to her previous six book-length narratives and are arranged in reverse chronological order, thus this book provides an insight into both the changes and the consistencies of Wattison's style and subject matter over thirty-five years.

From the title onwards, this is a collection replete with allusions – from high culture, especially literary, to fashion and popular culture. Part of the poet's procedure throughout much of this book is to travel with delight and poignancy through specific reference sets, but also to bed the work in contemporary contexts, which gather strength and power from the broader cultural touchpoints.

Wattison's is a poetry of flamboyant, associative weaving, of astute originality, of an imagination that can spin its balls high in the air and keep those trajectories surprising. Take, for example, the title poem, 'The Munchian O'. It is astounding for the transfiguring sophistication of its language and its ability to manoeuvre its way through a range of key political and literary aspects (Che Guevara, Neruda, Sartre, Auden) while decrying the ravages of war: in particular the children killed during the bombing of Aleppo, and the complacency that a never-ending news cycle and corrupt regimes can engender. The whole poem is a cry of suffering, against suffering and against the hollow responses of the West: 'The sallow gaping silent O covers its ears.' Wattison takes Munch's famous, pictorial mouth-wound and gives it context, voice and volume. Yet, the 'O' is also a cypher: as in 'Olvido' (I forget), as in 'orphans', as in the crass glitter of the West's materialism: 'The West Kardashian 5-million-dollar diamond *ring*' (my italics). This poem exemplifies Wattison's consummate ability to take a cultural gesture and make a profound, moving poem, using her references and erudition to expand and highlight. She's especially good at moving from a literary/

cultural perspective to a raw, hard-hitting one: '… the Munchian O/ of Syria's pulled-from-the-rubble, quail-ribbed, excoriated orphans…'

Intrinsic to the charm of this book is the way in which literature and culture are mixed in with the everyday. For Wattison the reading life is as significant as her family or social life, it is simply part of the complex matrix of living, responding, understanding. That's why she can confidently insert lines from a poem by Joseph Brodsky into her poem about apes in captivity ('The Apes Sang'), allowing the speaker to imagine the apes' lives in terms of Brodsky's musings on freedom and space, an existence beyond the routine and horror of captivity. It is also about the power of singing, of speaking up and speaking out. This engagement with Brodsky also makes it a powerful poem about exile.

For many writers their reading lives are as significant, perhaps even more so than their daily lives. For this is where the imagination thrives, exploring others' rhythms and ideas, gaining empowerment and inspiration from kinship with those for whom words and the craft of writing provide the most complex and concentrated response to human experiences. Wattison knows the power and joy of imaginatively entering the experiences of others and making them her own. One of the most delightful pieces in the volume, 'Better Boy, Early Girl and Green Zebra' describes a visit to a café (one of three such pieces, all full of luminous details) that serve teas named after literary figures. The list is engrossing and Wattison is playful and equally reverential and satirical: 'The list, like any anthology, is a confirmation by others, it's all warm and fuzzy herbal teas—if included. Brodsky is not there. I ask for his silvery, mulled *Exile* . . . It steams in whorls of Cyrillic'.

Wattison does not shy away from invoking (and evoking) her literary heroes. There are many poems in *The Munchian O* which pay homage to writers: Virginia Woolf, Saul Bellow, Sylvia Plath (almost a constant), Germaine Greer, William Carlos Williams to name some. Wattison delights in this dialogue, this exchange, this acknowledgement of affect and influence. This is a book that talks to other writers not in a scholastic or theoretical way, but in a way that is organic, imaginative and a natural consequence of her deep engagement with the writing life.

In 'If Life Has a Base That It Stands Upon' Wattison assumes the voice of Virginia Woolf writing a letter to Leonard Woolf. Here the language is fluid with detail, the water imagery powerful and suggestive, it's as if Woolf's voice has taken on the essence and power of water: 'The press of the tannin water is delicious, the bubbles that pummel and their persistent primordial green language . . . My leaden fur coat effervescing like an otter's, on end and electric.' The poem is a triumph of compassion and identification, of tonal and metaphorical authenticity.

The compassionate response comes through strongly also in her depiction of a visit to a zoo in 'A Peacock Sweeping', in which the speaker finds herself caught up in a boy's hyper-reactions to some of the animals they are viewing. The boy's manic energy is overwhelming, 'It is as though he has swallowed lightning', yet we are drawn into his enthusiasm and his animated responses in a way that is compelling and endearing. This is achieved through the changing energy of the syntax. Wattison skilfully embodies the boy's restless attention in her use of brief, sharp sentences, which she sets against the narrator's more sustained, complex and settled rhythms: 'My intention was to gaze at giraffes in silence. There is no silence. He adheres to me. The nervous giraffes distrust his animation, glide away, tongue at the trees. He asks why. We speak to the rhinoceros. I like its sooking, prehensile top lip, the short fringe of hair, like eyelashes, that edge its flicking ears; the bulk of it, the tender pink inside its mulching mouth.' Through her language and sentence structures the whole complexity of this human to human, human to non-human interaction is beautifully enacted and played out.

This poem, among others in the collection, reminds us of poetry's ability to bring us into a deeper awareness of ourselves and of others, and of our connections and responses to the non-human world. This is very powerfully evoked in the four-part poem 'Guernica 1–4' which depicts a lost and terrified dog running along a highway. The poem's repetitions and rearrangements of the same lines enact the relentlessness of the dog's frantic running. The poem is full of dramatic tension, of obsessive wondering and worry over the dog's fate—will it reach its destination, is there even a destination in mind, is the dog running towards something, or away from something, will it be struck by a vehicle? But the poem is more than just a description of an observed moment. The reference to 'Bede's sparrow' in the opening lines makes the dog's situation an allegory of our own, or indeed an allegory for all living creatures trying to survive outside the sanctuary of momentary safety. The questions about the dog's fate the poem poses are also questions which can be asked about our own, especially given the significance of the poem's title.

The existential cry, the Munchian O, recurs in many poems, yet there is diversity also, not only of content, but in form, from the prose pieces to the ribbon-like '45–47', or smaller, lyrical poems with their lilting undertow that will shift the reader towards an appreciation of the redemptive power of perception. Wattison's poems are always investigative, always humane. They are always willing to take risks. I know of no other Australian poet who writes quite like Meredith Wattison. She choreographs language in a way that is distinctive, deftly filtering moods and complex emotions through her uncanny vision as she aligns a deeply aesthetic mode of perception with the habitual and quotidian. Her language is sculptural and muscular, elegant and biting. Her music is both intense and playful, she can use the seductive registers of her voice to persuade and beguile, move and unsettle, but above all, her work is an enabling moral response to these complex times.

Judith Beveridge, 2019

Contents

The Munchian O
for John Hawke

'And what is Aleppo?'
American presidential candidate,
Gary Johnson, September, 2016

'The trucks and the food and the medicine just spontaneously
combusted. Anybody here believe that?'
US Secretary of State, John Kerry, addressing a UN Security
Council Meeting, challenging the indignant Russian Foreign
Minister, Sergei Lavrov's 'parallel universe', September 2016

'there is nothing poetic about a child whatsoever'
Simone de Beauvoir

After 'Musée des Beaux Arts' by W.H. Auden

Yes, that was me in the revolutionary belt; Che replicated, hung
    around my hips,
with beret, beard, cigar; without. A man behind me in the bus queue,
slicker than acronym, thought it was an opener.
I thought it buckled like the knees of his fellow med students,
those gathered sweetly, like pastries, in skirts, as Che read Neruda;
as Che, in sublimated Rolex, in philos. fatigues, anti-poetry,
    machismo, lucido, placido, simpático, lit Sartre's emulous cigar.
    Olvido.
A tongue and groove, an apostolic, a love knot of sorts, propagandist
florescence, this delicious poesy ring binds with a repeated line
like *Of earthli joyse thou art my choys* from that bow-lipped guerrilla.
It was the assassin's undressing, notch by lyrical notch. Me, cane field;
    you, machete.
A sustained loop, open milky circle, the Munchian O

of Syria's pulled-from-the-rubble, quail-ribbed, excoriated orphans,
    shock stilled,
the numb arc of chlorine barrel bombs and burn-to-the-bone,
set-teeth-chattering white phosphorous;
the un-extraordinary buckling breach, its tenuous orange blossom
and rose water ceasefire. (The sallow gaping silent O covers its ears.)
But Che, believe me, in this 24-hour-news-cycle, after 40, 45,
there is only the diabetic morsel, nymphets and waiting to die. It's a
    sickening dare
to drape your soul over a distracted love, repeatedly, during a
    prolonged season
of nimbus and abundance, like a sugar harvest.
The willing soul does not interest, there is no receipt of it, it is too
    like Sartre,
de Beauvoir and their great conscious cause; at all costs, and like
    a psychotic,
love; remember the Syrian sky, think of Auden's, of Bruegel's, feathers
    and boy,
falling unnoticed, as you catch (through your fingers) and
cast the crystallised stars above you, make syrup, blow and spin them
like an impartial confectioner, immune to blue sky, amandine distance,
reduction to numbers, complicity, the philosophical phosphorous O;
    the peace deal walkout. The West Kardashian 5-million-dollar
    diamond ring (and parted-lip, deific
selfie grille) crisis, O. Sympathique. Trajectoire. O.

World's End and Gadigal

for Lindy Morrison

I share a café table in Redfern with a young man whose bitten nails
are lacquered scarlet, or Hunter's Pink, like a London bus, then
roughly scraped at by his teeth. Let's call him Dorian. His hands
are large, pale and beautifully formed, their squareness implies both
invention and practicality, his alabaster thumbs arc like Bacon's. To
him it is androgynous transcendence; to me it is purely transport with
poetic nomenclatives, Monopoly's real estate; the stuff of desolate,
historical novels. It is Dickens sending his sons, cruelly burdened
with 'potential', to Australia, Austen on A Mystery Tour, the Brontës
looking for a rough gypsy or two. It is Blyton's imperious 'Parp-Parp'
taxonomy, Potter's Puddle-Duck's paisley shawl. (The 328 bus to
Chelsea, World's End, ran aground here, its deluded shoppers shuffled
through The Sales without a purse, or benefactor—but with grasping
hands. Some unleashed their European grotesques—the less callous
amongst them surprised themselves.) A man with cerebral palsy has
fallen crossing a lane and crawls into its gutter, a local man helps him
to his feet, leans him against a wall to regain his balance and checks
his forearms and bare legs for injury. He hugs his rescuer as though
he has pulled him from the sea. Heathcliff breaks from the man's
embrace, glowers and strides away, wolfhounds at his heels. Dickens's
sons gather after the fact. Dorian and I agree on, among other things,
Plath's delusions (her anglomaniacal brown study, sodden sheep, errant
cottage garden romanticism, for which I too have a propensity)—how
unfortunate they were for her, and how crucial it is to find someone
with illusions as real as your own and make them flesh. (Vivienne
Westwood described her 1965 'meeting' with Malcolm McLaren
as him being 'a one-off. He was fascinating and mad, and it was as
though I was a coin and he showed me the other side.' Its thrall lasted
fifteen years; at his 2010 funeral she wore a Gold Label headband, re
World's End unisex accessories, which stretched 'Chaos' across her

3

forehead, re his mantra re cash, re her lost protagonist.) Dorian hints at a discreet deep disappointment. (He and his full-lipped, saffron and chrome-haired girlfriend parted two months ago.) Dispossessed urban seagulls levitate and resist above us like metamorphosing plastic bags and our other side's intertwined other; mine has the blond shoulders, the flaxen fusilli, of the scrapped buffalo nickel, 'Liberty' on his flip side. (Horses bring their satin musculature to him, as I wake weighing words.) A worn meniscus rim, his proud man's good soldier's skin, flare at the Elysian edge of these feathered eclipses on Regent, just off Cope, beneath 2012's Transit of Venus, re her night-sweat fevers, Westwood's divine bustled cellulite, our hearts are high and rocked silent.

If Life Has a Base That It Stands Upon

(from Virginia to Leonard Woolf)

'If life has a base that it stands upon, if it is a bowl that one fills and fills and fills—then my bowl without a doubt stands upon this memory.'

Virginia Woolf, 'A Sketch of the Past', 1939

Darling Mongoose,
    I know a love letter is expected of me and we both know that our Victorian childhoods made little animals of us. And dearest L., another I have written has been fed upon, pawed over, sniffed at on the slab—
where I liken myself to a ball in a fountain, and she the fountain.
I tell the Dearest Creature about my fried heart. And your delicate, handwrought invitation from the mandrill (very nearly in a debossed sharp Hebrew)—
to view her very private exhibition, her jutting fuzzed heliotrope on display—that too, sniffed at. A love letter is superfluous when love is the greenish light dipping its toes
into this dragging river with its streaming, radiating weeds, maceration, transmutation, sift and scrape. The press of the tannin water is delicious, the bubbles that pummel and their persistent primordial green language. All is carbon and trace percentages, our marriage's existentialism, water, my floating amber beads loose and fluid as gender, context and impulse. My leaden fur coat effervescing like an otter's, on end and electric; tiny filmy, jelling things overwhelm it, spawn, leafy fish sing in Greek, lip my pearls, distend, extol at my earrings. Were you there in the garden, with your loamy ashes (and mine), when the Australian poet pulled an apple from our tree and ate it? I wished it could have been a honeyed—or pickled—fig for her; fine white river sand its grit. I had floated above it like a snagged silk scarf, though my eyes closed, I could see every abrading grain; all I could think about was my trembling Mongoose reading my letter

5

and suddenly my first spinning memory. My thin ring glinted and slipped from me like a bent yellow ogee, obliqued and weightless, a gilding for the silt, its molecular trace of the slavers' Egypt. My lost Roman brooch there too, the one I lost in 1921—on March 10th— and dropped into *Jacob's Room*, a garnet in an orchard, and in *To The Lighthouse*, as a weeping willow, set with pearls, on a beach. Its existence didn't depend on my possession of it. It did seem smaller. So too, my bookbinding tools, still in their canister, flint arrow-heads and Shakespeare's father's glover's shears (often pawned)—or two elver picnic knives crossed? Elizabethan nails. Swans swam above like repelling suspended spheres, magnetic dark clouds.

Who were the ancients who believed that (we as) bears were born without a definite form and licked into shape by their mothers? The Greeks? The Victorians? The Stephens? You'll remember my mother's last six metered words to me were—hold, yourself, straight, my, little (&) Goat—as I slipped out through their door, the door to the sexual centre of the house, to our conception and births, to their deaths and then, to where?—into all that black crape?—is that where we went? We lived within an eclipse of shocks; warm towels, a drop of brandy in warm milk, the planets of sleep.

That orbiting (sleeping like a top) first memory of the black ground of a dress my mother wore, we were on a train or an omnibus and I sat on her lap. There were blots of colour, red, purple and blue, I think anemones, then connected to this is hearing the little acorn on the nursery blind, in St Ives, drawn across the floor as the wind blew the blind out. I have described (satisfactorily to myself) its intensity. I heard the green sea; the drawn acorn, I saw the yellow light; the blind's exhalation. I could only describe my thoughts as gratitude to be there and of a pure animal ecstasy connected to the excitement of a journey.

Then at fifteen, I was a nervous, gibbering monkey in the same cage as my father, a morose lion. I would still hear the tinkling of my mother's twisted silver bracelets as she moved about the house; remember her three rings, a diamond, an emerald, an opal (whose pinkish lights would fix my eyes to the lesson book she taught us from)—which I gave to you, dearest L. for your hominid finger.

As a child I remember, again in St Ives, fighting on the lawn with Thoby—our fists! I stopped and let him beat me. Of course, Thoby gave me you—he thought your tremor violent, savage and sublime. And so did I.

Only you would relish the mandrill's display, only you could smooth all this with impeccable punctuation, knew my abbrevs., would fold my black anemone gloves into vanilla pod monkey fingers, find my dew wet things and know.

I hear our dogs barking and there is suddenly, again, my first blurred memory, anemones, and this—dearest Nessa and I used to wear brightly printed cotton florals, as though dressed by Gauguin. We were accused of wildness and nakedness in Bloomsbury; those colours the colours on the black ground of my mother's close dress, the journey to the base that life, if a bowl, has stood upon and *one fills and fills and fills.*

You have been its trembling fill; the blind's drawing acorn; are now this tannin water; my context always.

Your trembling toes dipping and my tiny hooves and nubbly horns—I am aware that to wake as a goat is to own no property—will take me gasping, climbing, a clean little slate with a high round brow, from this river—the sharp bow of my thick billy hips dips and tilts equally as your fill, rocking with the impulsive stepped rhythm of writing. I know the mongoose will kindly endure, to the onlooker, my

7

weightless comedy; let me eat their roses, sleep by the fire, will hear a third voice and will not make a vellum of me.

This has been, and remains, our carbon parable.

Yr.
Mandy, V.

Baxter Boots and Julia Margaret Cameron

The purest elements enter by particle; dark matter,
I am rushing—have pulled on a pair of black tights;
as I favour the left,
that done, right toes reach down
into a gritted curve,
I pinch and readjust and pull on my Baxter's.
As I will be walking from The Cross, through
Woolloomooloo to The Domain I will suffer these grains,
so I pull off my right boot, stand on one leg,
and with my right leg and foot out
fail to find any impediment in the toe,
so I turn the leg inside out—nothing—
I redress, step forward—eureka—
it has dropped into my left boot
and I accept the pure irony of rushing to see
the cracked collodion negative of allegory,
sunlight's intransience, accepted flaw, Cameron's own scratches;
the portrait of Darwin's bricked brow,
wan Julia Jackson, Duckworth, Stephen/
Virginia Woolf's transparent mother,
her neck, porcelain; her Warholian, Pre-Raphaelite's tilted
martyr's gaze, a non-binary nude cupid's swan wing prop taken,
Alice Liddell full-fledged, the precision of distant gravity in
    exactness, drop;
lives are made so.

The Film Student's Shoes

Under the sole of each size 12 shoe is a large egg-shaped hole. The lost layers grade inwards to a clean pared edge. Cross-legged, his proof of purchase on Sydney's streets, footpaths, lanes and alleys shows itself. His polished uppers mislead; his heels are barely worn. He walks his odyssey as the crow flies. As in Chartres, there are no pilgrims without shoemakers. No festivals without students. These Portuguese, pragmatically buffed boots I wear were bought almost two years ago, though I live in a softer place. They are in the style of Magritte's cleft chestnut. I ask about each cameo. One shoe is lined with a black leather coin purse, I guess with the zip removed, the other with a piece of cardboard from a pizza box. I ask if anything is written on it—no. He also recommends cardboard from microwave meals. Ingenuity, creativity and make-do cannot be learnt though I would prefer the incorporation of a word. I did notice that the release/disappearance of his institutionalised/despondent magician was achieved wordlessly and in one rising shot. I see him the following day, it is raining, the makeshift has shifted and his socks have similar cameos. The soles of his feet experience the osmosis of puddled bitumen, concrete and the cinema's stepped swathe of garish carpet. I offer him a pair of shoes I have bought for him. He disdains, will not accept their square-toed, corporate conformity. He prefers a point. I had thought it a pointed square. He does not budge. I give him two coin purses and quip, in case of emergency. One holds enough to buy a pair of shoes, or line one instep. The other is merely shoe leather. I return the superfluous shoes without question, or the offer of enlightenment, with proof of purchase. There is no interest in why; only the exchange of filmy blue lucre.

Outside of Jacob's Room

'Friday, April 8th. 10 minutes to 11 A.M. (1921)

And I ought to be writing Jacob's Room; and I can't, and instead I
shall write down why I can't—this diary being a kindly blankfaced old
confidante. Well, you see, I'm a failure as a writer. I'm out of fashion:
old: shan't do any better: have no headpiece: the spring is everywhere:
my book out (prematurely) and nipped, a damp firework.'

Virginia Woolf,
A Writer's Diary

I lug my drum into the danse macabre; *The Woolfian Encyclopaedia of*
Light and The Eye, the full set.
I read, therefore I amp.

(We pass by the spires of)
Oxbridge, Camford, Oblivion's
Periphery-on-Sea.

Fewer than, not less, my raked, unequalled love.
I am quite a different animal now,
my eyesight failing.

Jacob Flanders' shoes hang above the glaring crossing
like polished leathern pears, dusted with Italy.
Their wilting stems tightly knotted together like a dropped
    black glove.

Three Ethnic Bangles and a Tin Lotus Box

It is the making of things that interests me, the dimension of their materials. It is the sifting of objects through value systems, their provenance and discovery amongst the West's excess and detritus in charity shops and flea markets. A delicate buffalo horn bangle has a gloss, and a weight, which delights me. Its feel against my skin is warmly organic and its striations, although (echidna) quill-like and various when curled into a ring, are traces and telling like strata and the growth rings of a tree. Its polish and smoothness is gentle industry and care. It is quietly perfect. An oval tribal bangle is thinly banded by tightly wound (onto a core of Nigerian vine), vivid yellow and blue threads of (found? re-purposed?) plastic, and intricately woven into white-on-black checkerboard lozenges, a white stranded square between them. It is weightless and the size of a man's wrist. It sits like a breath against my skin; like tradition and sure-fingered, commercial adaptation. I wear it sleeping. A heavy bone bangle, which puts me onto the premises and into the presence of Judith Beveridge's 'The Bone Artisan', is fitted with a bespoke silver metal hinge and pinned clasp, and is the creamy colour of ivory. Again, striated and traced. A partly lost cinnabar pigment has been applied to its flat polished surface. There is lighter, rougher tooling within it. It has both the thoroughness and inventiveness of poverty. There is, respectfully and economically, no wastage from a carcass, it has the ethic of those who pick through hospital waste and trade in the collection, reuse and misuse of plastics as a cottage industry. It is heavy on my arm. I wear the three together. In the same small cane basket (its contents a mostly plastic tangle; a race day's gauzy fascinator, with orange polyester poppy, in the mix) there was a wide, cloth wristband with rows of heavy, roughly cast, small, round, brass bells sewn to it. It secured with a bright, small square buckle and a thin, brown leather strap cut from a satchel. It whispered hybridisation, movement and music; ritual. I hold a small, smooth, tin object. It is swollen like a pumpkin. It warms in my hand, fits into my palm like a pebble. It has been engraved and oxidised, with tiny silvered and gilt flowers. In its centre is a circle of rings. I buy it blind, unaware that it splits and is a box. Its layers of embellishments are bread and butter stock-in-trade, the melting down of other objects, child labour. The raised tin within it, its inverted creases, shows a more botanic realism—its base of roots, a rust of unspecified residue. Its warm roundness somehow fits my recent days of gently pushing a split antibiotic tablet down into the throat of a dingo/collie cross early mornings, late afternoons. The shared split moment of innate mistrust, and then of trust favoured, sifts and polishes, makes a quietly creative, Western, gesture of us.

A Peacock Sweeping

The boy; the boy tap dances and somersaults for the duration of
the early morning, two-hour tour. It is as though he has swallowed
lightning for breakfast. He experiences everything sevenfold. 'Oh!
Look at that!' Striped lemurs huddle around a sun lamp, wrap their
arms, legs and tails around each other. A digesting knot of African
wild dogs sleeps around a tree. Biblical coil-horned goats stand
on their silky beards. There's a Jericho reference. 'Feel this tree! So
smooth!', as he brushes past me, kicking up his heels, half-turning,
arms ascendant. He gets emotional. 'There's blood on the camel!' The
camel has caught itself on the cyclone fencing. It is part hosed-cement
nativity; its nimbus evaporating. Its eyes bucolic; fudge-brown. Its shut
nostrils miraculous. There are an estimated one-million feral camels
in Australia. We learn the camel is one of the most efficient animals;
it makes very little shit. This cheers him. My intention was to gaze at
giraffes in silence. There is no silence. He adheres to me. The nervous
giraffes distrust his animation, glide away, tongue at the trees. He asks
why. We speak to the rhinoceros. I like its sooking, prehensile top
lip, the short fringe of hair, like eyelashes, that edge its flicking ears;
the bulk of it, the tender pink inside its mulching mouth. He likes
its steaming rhino shit. The boy's mother has mastered a detached
indifference as some on the tour outwardly tire of him. She too was
emotional about the camel. The boy as parrot, her parrot, is intensely
interested and speaks gently to the apes he wants to photograph. He
asks them to sing; they will not, they do not ape. He sings. They do
not play the game. He asks them to look at him, to lift their chins;
they do this. 'Thank you', he says. He is given a voucher from a staffer
for doing/saying this. The hippopotamus sleeps standing with its face
in the mud. The hippopotamus, annually, is the most responsible
animal in regards to human deaths. They do not like to be disturbed in
the water. Our volunteer guide is wonderfully patient with the boy. She

involves him in a presentation about the scrub turkey; she is impressed by this bird, admires its tenacity. The boy is amazed by how deeply the male buries the eggs in a mounded earth nest; and the ventilation, and all the variations of, needed to create both sexes; and the bird's over-estimation of its size regarding predators. The boy terrorizes the meerkats with his enthusiasm. He wakes the nocturnals. Agrees to put down the stick. There are stories of missing primates and sedative-laced, pink-iced donuts being left in high, strategic places. The zoo is yet to open. The boy is yet to catch breath. I will queue to feed the giraffes at ten-fifteen. Their sweet civility; a slimy purple tongue pulling my fingers into a rough mouth sates me. A peacock sweeps the café floor and suddenly spans, pulses and thrums, and just as suddenly goes back to sweeping. The boy takes off his hat. It is musical theatre.

The Apes Sang

It is a deep, yet removed, singing. It begins with whoops, howls; ends
in moans. The bigger their audience (intrusion), the louder their song.
It is a madrigal, Magnum Mysterium, da capo. A return to blank,
barefaced silence is their digression. The apes sang, though not to, or
for, us. Their full throat sacs send their songs skyward. If they could
know one poem, then let it be a Brodsky. His 'Advice To A Traveller';
they would need no other and no other poet. But they must plot
from the confines of the brown paper bags thrown onto their island
at feed times. They must doubt the swing ropes, the leafless arbour,
their keepers' clockwork oars. They must learn to distrust variously cut
fruits and popcorn, to mournfully tear open the missives like the old
female. She must remember the mountains. Where: *'If you must creep,*
then creep.' Where: *'Standing up, you lie flat. Which suggests your true/*
freedom's in falling down. That's the way, it appears,/to conquer, once in
the mountains, vertigo, raptures, fears.'
> (And how she first stood to see over the tall grasses and began
> walking.)
> And the plateau where:

'. . . when you shudder at how infinitesimally small you are,
remember: space that appears to need nothing, does
crave, as a matter of fact, an outside gaze,
a criterion of emptiness—of its depth and scope.
And it's only you who can do the job.'

only you who can do the job.

Translated from the Russian by the author (Joseph Brodsky)
and George L. Kline
© 1989 by Joseph Brodsky
Farrar, Straus and Giroux, Inc.

Rewilding

Down through the deep aisles of an organic grocer's is a wild foods
café. The waitstaff wears crepuscular black and Mexican silver
jewellery. They hand out the menu like a new translation of an
explicit, sacred text. 'Specials' an errata. Juicers and blenders chirr.
A booming voice rises from a sunny corner, 'Australia!, the socialist
paradise; everyone expects backup!' He wears a power shirt of wide
stripes, its cuffs upturned, once. He viscerally, still, hates Gillard;
loves the box joke still. A Saturday's Herald expert. His fine Panama
intimates a Conran lampshade. His rough, somehow goatish dog is
tethered to a chair, it looks as though it has been to a salon, its fur
the colour of Burberries, crouching to tenant the chair, encumbered,
its little black accessories graze the pavers. There is a monkey made
from wire on each table, the table number hangs on a disk from an
ear. They are all on all fours, their body surface is filled with tiny
brown, burnishing glass beads threaded onto wire. I think of the
fingers of their makers, and of those who once picked cotton. Some
of the monkeys wear pink crowns, some have silver wings. Their eyes
are black glass marbles, their mouths empty grins; no sharp teeth
or pointed tongues. Some tails have been twisted into coils, some
doubled into a handle. A similar gold lion, though loudly eccentric,
hovers above the barista. A multicoloured and grimacing, attenuated
giraffe at the cashier; through its open mouth is a completely empty
body. These are like the animals colonial artists drew—a default for
the familiar, animals never actually seen. Koalas/possums deemed
monkeys. A frail dog beneath a table becomes hysterical at the
approach of someone known. I witness the rapturous authenticity
of a leaping heart. The American accent of a young woman cuts
through the courtyard. Her talk is trivial and joyous. I'll have an
organic skim cap. I'll eat nothing. It is too warm, too early in the
day, for sweet potato and coconut soup. Next door they sell ride-ons.

A proximate chain saw erupts and murmurs. On the other side is a car park. 'Look—a flyer for a Women's Drumming Group!', a father/partner/husband affectedly shouts. She self-consciously acknowledges and saunters past the lentils, palm sugar and lecithin. Their children possess. He buys something foil-packed and expensive and leaves without it. He is elsewhere and comfortable. Their daughter, in a pretty, shirred sundress, slowly and reverently curtsies between tables, perhaps she is 'being' Mary Donaldson. The son wants something loudly. Something within reach and inappropriate, involute; something raw and politically sound, unprocessed and unpaid for. One small shoe is thrown. Single, middle-aged children with their ailing, remaining parent, roam and eventually settle at tables in half-sun, half-shade, away from smokers and children. Appetites nil. Before hacked Africa and zoos, the sinuous, heavy-headed
baboon sat at the gates of the underworld.

Rewild

I sit at table 8. I know this because there is a numbered disk hanging
from a glass bead and wire monkey's tail. It sits on the table with a
small, delicate white bowl of sea salt. This monkey wears a crown of
tiny pink beads, with larger gold beads in a row of six up its centre
and across its peaks. It has large pink eyes and a face, or mask, of tiny
gold beads. Due to rain, table 8 is pushed into a corner against the,
usually open, thick glass partition. I sit on a padded bench, which
runs the length of the allotted eating area in this passionately organic
large space. The outside tables and chairs are stacked in a dry corner.
Their numbered monkeys are hooked, in a row, by their legs, over the
horizontal edge of a folded table. Their tails in the air like a naturist
cancan. Flooded grey pavers glint and reflect shrubbery and a ghostly,
heritage-listed, reset set of hewn beams that tautly tilt and skew a
pooling shade sail of aqueous liquors. There are two men opposite me
in a passionate exchange about 'next week'. The staff are fractured,
coffee and cake seems complicated. There is a din. They offer a slow,
chatty service, nightly cooking classes and a naturopathic dispensary.
A chalkboard above the servery is almost Hebraic with a platitude
about happiness. A plate comes garnished with something crimson
and unknown and sliced kiwi. I also eat its fur. There is a little boy
spinning in circles near me, a little car in each hand. His mother and
companion, next to me, in diamonds and designer clothes, loudly
discuss just how long it will take for someone to speak to you in
this town, before anyone knows you, and how having kids helps the
process. They could afford and wear Dame Westwood's perfect, plaid
Anglomania tailoring, but not her manifesto, her one-thousand-and-
one interrelated decisions about silk, technique and resistance. His is
the ideal tousle of flaxen corkscrews. He is a beautiful child in oversize
OshKosh. Exhausted, exasperated, he stands in the open doorway and
pees through his baggy, striped pants onto his rain boots. Her reaction

is nervous, slow and falsely calm. She does not wish to irrevocably damage his male psyche and changes his offending clothes in the courtyard. I speak, 'It could be worse.' She ignores the little puddle he has made. Those entering and leaving through this ancillary door, like fairies, spread his DNA through these exotic, organic aisles, through this town. His trajectory of rich, white privilege has begun. He returns to the table and drives his little cars through a monkey's legs, beneath its belly and out the other side. And again. Sometimes he crashes them together. His mother reaffirms that he is wonderful and that he has made a bridge. My coffee card is clipped as though I am travelling. After nine coffees the next is free.

Better Boy, Early Girl and Green Zebra

It is the end of autumn. Small fringed jacquard blankets are folded
over the backs of the outside chairs, whose riveted, tube-aluminium
frames arc in the intense, but cold, sunlight. They are travel rugs for
the unmoving, the unmoved. Or a series of forgotten tweedy beach
towels, their swimmers long overdue, their tentative presence, unlike
the sunglasses of German tourists, is no longer a territorial claim.
Or a tablecloth for a cold table, teacups with cold feet, a surface to
play Snap on or for makeshift ironing, a heavy hot teapot, creased
shirttails. I would wish to wear three. To tie one around my waist at
one hip, one behind my neck and wrap one around my head, like
a towel for my hair, twisted and tucked under at the back. I would
epitomise a free and easy negativism in a tightly scripted musical scene
in a 1950s American movie. Although the use of heliotrope, eau-de-
nil or grenadine silk curtains would be wilder to acquire. Astaire on
drums. A striped necktie threaded through his belt loops. Thus he
is anti-establishment, antigravity. He wears perfect, banded socks.
Trepanned jazz for a white audience, rated G. Somehow, suddenly I
would be wearing dyed satin dancing shoes. The crouching wire table
monkeys remain bare. Recently departed sitters have restyled their
tails. Coils are now at sharp angles, some almost detached and tweaked
erect like wide-eyed lemurs' bristling striped flags. Leaping like lords.
One's tip of its tail is in its mouth. Some are strung together thus so.
Some crouch for others. The list of mainly teas is cheeky and various.
I mention merely a few. We could sip on a *Frank Harris*, a camomile
and Viagra blend. A *Nin's Saddle* is chocolate laced with chilli. There
is *The Wilde Geranium*, 'a punishing sweet red blend'. The *Toklas
Stein* is a rosebud and French Vanilla infusion, also known as *Alice B.
Gert*, *Picasso With Hair* or *Come To Tea*. 'If you like this, you'll also
like *Lawrence's Fig*, recommended for secluded picnics.' There is *The
Lone Woolf*, 'best served cold', it is simply river water with a glittery

scoop of grit and pebbles. *Slessor's Bells* is oily, black and reflective, with anise and licorice. *Kafka's Tram* shyly steeps through pleats. The *Joseph Roth* 'the clouded brew of angels' is also known as *Blue-eyed Soul* or *The Hofmann Translation*. *Beckett's quaquaquaqua* is also known as *Mondrian's Green*. *Hughes's Bruises* is endorphin, pheromone, fox fur, nettle and dock. The *Wuthering Plath* 'is like being mailed into space'. *Fallada's Postcard* arrives surreptitiously. And new to the swelling and mostly predictable list, there is simply, *The Patrick White*, 'hallucinatory and clarifying', purported to 'sharpen eyesight, empathy, sagacity and the tongue'. Not recommended for vegetarians. Also becoming known as the *Black and Blue White* or *The Squattocrats' Sweet Boy*. (There is a small herd of Schleich goats on the windowsill. Its morose billy is white-bearded, long-eared and encumbered by airbrushed sweetmeats. White and Lascaris bred goats, and dogs, and grew flowers, fruit and vegetables at Castle Hill. I think he would enjoy this gambol—the solid little piece of plastic has the reverb of a mandala—the recounts of my thunderclap conversion and fidelity, my celebratory underlinings of all those pleasant shocks.) *The Constant Garner* (or *Hel's Bells* when poured into cones made from pages of the dailies) 'hearty', 'refines experience'. The list, like any anthology, is a confirmation by others, it's all warm and fuzzy herbal teas—if included. Brodsky is not there. I ask for his silvery, mulled *Exile*. It comes in the familiar shoe-shaped ladle. It steams in whorls of Cyrillic. 'an outside gaze' floats and skates on its surface in tiny pasta letters. I collect them in an enamelled teaspoon. *Bellow's Gift*, with crocus and saffron is not there. The quintessentially Australian *Editors' Acrostic*, also known as *The Blackball, Pedant's Gulp, Ern's Turn* or *Ern's Burn* has been pulled also. It's a stewed astringent blend. Also used as a thinner and was once used as a pungent marinade for mutton. I cover my knees with a fringed blanket. I wrap my shoulders. Ripe polyphonic sparrows erupt in the hedge. A little sweetheart walks through wearing her thick dressing gown, pyjamas and sheepskin slippers. A white ribbon is tied in her neat, wavy bob. She and her father buy takeaway coffees. She chats to the waitstaff unselfconsciously. She is excited to be out early. Another little girl, all ready for the school day, has nervously crossed the room by herself to choose a book for her mother to read to her. She is pink-cheeked with triumph. Her hair is flyaway. A little boy is spooning scrambled egg into the pocket of his red Parka while his father builds a tower with blocks on the table. The boy has hidden several paper sachets of sugar under a chair, out of view of his over-zealous parents. He is ready for leaner times. He slips the spoon and the sugar into his boot. The salads here are presented under a cloche as though foraged. They are dressed with moonlight and dew and seem to have been nibbled at by alpaca and lambs. They are garnished with slow bees, twigs with lichen, tufts of alpaca wool, clover and wild violets. Tomato cultivar choices are nefarious. From Adoration, Beef Steak, Better Boy, Big Beef, Big Rainbow, Coeur De Boeuf, Early Girl, Enchantment, Green Zebra, Mc Dreamy, Moneymaker, Mr Stripey and Traveller I choose Better Boy, Early Girl and Green Zebra. They are crushed and squeezed and thoughtfully placed amongst nasturtiums and torn crisp Icebergs. Gems of pomegranate are gingerly added. There is a soupçon and smear of risky fungi, a crumble of goat's cheese, a drizzle of cold pressed extra virgin olive oil, a line of honey. It is known that these purists encourage the addition of homegrown oranges. We are expected to bring them and gently peel them with our hands, there is no peeler, no knife, and to add their autonomous segments to our plates. It is a meditation. I do so. The use of cutlery is not encouraged. Suddenly we are sucking at, teething, tonguing and spitting pomegranate seeds. We do it with the expertise of spider monkeys. Our little eyes and delicate fingers are so easily lent to embroidery, watchmaking and surgery. The warm pear salad, *The Whiteley*, is three salted brown-skinned pears arranged and presented on sand. Both White and Whiteley ate with their eyes. I speak to a man who has watched me here for months. He has decided that today is the day to speak. He delivers international racehorses. He has, on need, had to cut into the tarpaulin, which covers a stall, and climb in with a horse that had panicked and flipped itself over on takeoff after the first refuel. He always has a series of needles to administer in case of emergency, i.e. the need to sedate or the need to *Green Dream* (euthanize). He had to force himself under the horse to prop its head so it wouldn't choke itself. He had to sedate it steadily and heavily. He lay there with it for hours covered in foam, blood and shit. He arrived in Dubai with dead leg. He tells me about the rough bristling horse he cried against when his brother's baby son died. Perhaps this is the true function of poets and horses. We are told things. He is known in the industry, and paid accordingly, for his kindness. He catches foals when standing, birthing mares choose gravity. A couple walk through wearing hemp and Hilfiger. They are salmon milkers. A delivery of warm bread is wheeled through, its bearer, going at a clip through bent bands of sun and shadow, grins keen. Coins in his green pockets like giddyup.

Response to John Hawke's Poem,
'The Demolition of Hotel Australia'
(reading Patti Smith in a Hailstorm)

I've had the ice chandelier installed, the installers, too, are ice; on ice.
    I sit
beneath it reading a roaming woman's words, she writes of the
    mystical nausea
between dreaming and waking. My tiny chiffon hat, a leek-green
    bromeliad, reluctantly fitted by Seidler with nylons and wire,
    plunks and plinks; is architecture cocked
for restorers and frothing aspic frogs; Delphic and plangent
    as hailstones,
John. Snugglepot and Cuddlepie identify as gamine; with Hepburn
    and Caron. Skippy looks concerned and dismembered.
    P. L. Travers adopts me. Nick Cave asks Skip
about the Glass piano in the archive. Geoffrey Rush walks through
    Lear's storm
soliloquy in a porkpie, walking a small saltwater.

Sequential Agency

It was on Southwark Station, Jubilee Line,
on the ascending escalator,
a well-known actor stood behind me.
I wanted to turn and say,
'I saw you in something—
you was a righ' nuh'uh!',
but I couldn't remember
what 'something' was
or his name,
and he looked edgy
and exposed
and I meant to praise.

Outside,
a rangy fox
turns the dimming car park
splendid,
jogs my memory
with its loose, low tail lit,
its wayward carriage—
quite something –
a loving, struggling father in Dr Who,
his anxious son generated
a subconscious portal,
young Ronnie Biggs,
Atonement –
you found the lead a place to sleep
at Dunkirk
and went through his pockets

with the wild, diverted face
of an angel; sequential agency.
Visceral as the envied, desired sister's
green silk liquescence.

And like the Tate Modern's
foggy rows of silver birches,
seemingly, like us, attached like Kafka's,
on that and this graphite morning,
these distant things follow.

Buy Asters (December 1996, Dunblane, Scotland)

He said,
'Buy asters
because the rabbits
won't eat them.'

The graves
will be a sweet,
nauseating mauve,
and inedible.

The rabbits track a snow
of desperate grief, delicately,
barely touching the ground
like children,
and barely hungry;
they move out
to gardens
at night,
frozen
at my approach on foot,
leaning into hedges, and
almost green in the foggy white
    of a stranger's headlights.
    A deer approaches
    from the corner, breathing for me.

Head of a Man

In the river,
the head of a man,
in a piece of cloth,
in a plastic bag
in mangroves.
It was dropped,
they say,
from the bridge
and found here.
Why, when I was told,
did I say,
'It doesn't surprise me.'?

because when I have
walked there,

where the grey, gulping mud
is spiked with the upthrust breathing roots,
    I have looked
for such a thing.

That mud, that black water,
that ultra, deep green,
its tides' slough
of aluminium, paper, glass, plastic, wood, rubber
is always daubed
with that black,
smiting water.

The river fills his mouth with more than teeth and tongue.
Landscape and throat open-ended, a serrated blade of sky.

Germaine's Postcard

Her handwriting is full-looped,
large, feminine, connected, unconnected,
the t's cross, the i's dot
trails. Mind is quick. The bottom curve of her s
twists into the o of my name
like an 8, continuous, steady as wire, neon tubing,
passion vine. The o's twin in 'sisterhood'
hangs like a clear (Monarch) butterfly egg.
Her signature is nervure, is the pen
slipping, skipping
as a finger on a wet window.
The brand name stamped
on the inside of the crisp, textured
envelope is
conqueror®.

The sweet analogy is not lost on me.
Even Boadicea wrote like a girl.

Votive

The ritual begins by filling a plastic basin with warm water. It is carried
from the bathroom to the bedroom. It is placed firstly on a stool, then
on to the floor. Soap and a flannel cloud the water. My hands bathe
the woman who has removed her nightie. She sits with a sense of calm
and pained skin's need for pleasure. It is like bathing a tired child. I
lift her arms, we speak quietly of shared things. This true intimacy
is purifying. We have forgotten the things that have strained and
estranged us. These mornings our bond is primitive. These days are
bordered by routine. I am preparing her for death. I am pleasing her
prickling skin. I dry her. I treat her skin with lotions and oils. Liver
cancer has swollen her body into a state of pregnancy, distension,
emaciation. Life is bursting from the dark soil of March. I have
travelled from Autumn to Spring, from Sydney to Northern Scotland
to bathe her. The liver was once thought to exude love and courage.
The ritual ends with a fresh nightie, accommodating pillows, a
flowered quilt. She rests.
Other mornings we, a nurse and I, walk her to the bathroom. She
removes her nightie and walks naked through the house, we are fully
clothed, unholy. Her physical weakness rushes her. We battle to steady
her, keep the syringe driver (morphine) untangled, unstrained, and
keep up with her, our reaching hands and arms taking her weight. Her
swollen legs and feet grip her. I have prepared the bath for her, run
warm water beneath her bath seat. We shift her across it until she is
centred. We turn her, lift and lower her feet into the pleasure of the
warm water. She visibly relaxes. I push my hand between her thigh
and the hinge that lifts as the seat is lowered, to spare her a pinch or a
bruise.
She can stand the sinking until it forces her to sit upright. We stop
its descent. She sits, this morphed woman, alabaster grace perched on
vinyl with her fingers in her ears, as I reverently wash her hair. I tip

water over her head, down her back like a bowed-head statue. She is the praying figure in a fountain; a Gothic ideal, a Medieval Eve. The nurse and I are two of the Danaides, we perpetually pour water over this veiled woman. We are myth personified. We are trying to fill a sieve with water.

London, April 5th, 2005

My son
scraped the soles of his shoes
all the way across
your Millennium Bridge.
Its surface resonant, strings,
ridges, embossed.
London, he played you
like a blackboard,
a trembling-toe, undulant
washboard.
A small group
of vibrating Australians
breach your Arts Board's
Modern Tate. Our frequency vespertine.
Beneath us a bamboo whistler
murders a bird, a suited Grayson Perry
articulates, will commit to clay.
My brother-in-law
hears it across the river
on Upper Thames'
harmonic shore.
Each discordant note
murders another.
Millennia mere tremors
there. Vikings,
unheard.
Detonation and siren
on spate. Axe heads
deeper. Located by sonar,
the physics of a child's
refractory foot.

Albatross

In Australia
our bodies travel light,
we do not sardine.
Here I know
the difficulty
of peeling
one's arms
of downy sleeves,
the improbability
of room to extend enough
to amend enough skin
(for heat release)
without infringing,
without impinging
on your fellow passengers'
space.
I remove my coat
like a zippered straightjacket
and hold it on my lap
like an albatross.
The elegant black man's suit,
across from me,
is lifting, effortless flight;
its wingspan minutely tailored by
herringboned filaments and Paul Smith's
coat of arms' six-sleeved literal graphic.
My six arms do not fly—
I think of Bondi, as updraft.

Volition

My generosity extends
to the dog sleeping on the bed
between us, as fidelity,
yours (generosity)
does not extend
of its own volition,
it allows,
does not invite,
kisses me once
as it slaps,
benignly,
the dog's rump
thrice.

God Enough

For God's sake,
take your clothes off,
get into bed with me
and let's shape each other
into the gods we need.
Riding, thin-skinned,
as vicariously
as need be.
My tongue deep in your mouth
like that tired, two-edged
question of fullness,
lustrous, dark, god enough.
It tastes (omnipotent)
equal love. No skin between us.
Unutterably, gloriously,
skinless.
I am panting the woman's prayer.
You grip, scale, man's deliverance.
Our achievements, or no,
of our days
are ignored by these gods;
they care little for worldliness
and nothing for perfection
or ruin.

Grmmr, Rhtrc, Lgc

The order of the pattern
by which we place
the laws of disenvowelled
txts

is the flirtation,
the iambic prize,
the glyphics
that fix

the mind's
open green pastures
buzzing, winging, with mice,
spreading like Latinate love and grief.

In Defence of the Illiterate Ancients

Words,
their iron-fisted spelling,
their free address,
their spilling,
must be seen
to come from
a mouth,
must cloud
a dull mirror at least,
must be caught or grown, wear nothing.

Lamb-limbed

She is anathema to fences,
civility, vassalage,
horseflesh.
She is spectacle,

double Colossus;
four legs planted
like a splaying,
iron-legged table.

Anti-gravity,
she is Pity's horse,
tail like a
twisting flame.

She is birth furnace,
Blake's Tyger.

Is she from the like of her foal?

This golden synergy
is Nebuchadnezzar's
night forest
bright a.m.

symmetry of that volcanic,
heart-shaped bellows
and its like again.

And its like again
drops to earth
lamb-limbed
as a folded hand.

Corporeally vitreous,
vitreously incorporeal,
the body a poverty,
real and unreal
to the eye.

Slipping in the afterbirth,
we will struggle to empty
the foal's brazed bowel

to bring it
to our gossamer-gloved worship
and lambskin bridle.

Matron in Lime*

Dear Sir,
now that I no longer
think of you,
wait,
or want,
I can see
that these past
dozens of months
have seen me transform
from skinned animal (desire)
to animal skin.
Please accept this last(ing) gift.
Thank you once again,
for the opportunity
to study, at close quarters,
this blind animal.
Please, no thoughts
of taxidermy;
the eyes are never right;
its joy incalculable.
And I would know
that it is stitched
with my own hair,
by my own hand
and its animal bare.
Steep it in lime's
milky wash
until it is
wash itself.
I will wear soft leathers;
pink and tan gloves.
A chartreuse, Rodinesque veil.

Breasts in cool cabbage leaves,
cabochon citrine nipples.
Chalky clay and olive oil
about my waist,
mons,
(arms, knees, calves, feet,
the back of me),
thighs in amber.
Toes pistachio.
Asparagus spiking beneath my heels.

I (tartly) mourn painlessness
and self-containment only.

(My painstaking, detailed illustrating
is like Miss Potter; at best,
transfixed at the frozen swill bucket;
at worst, a (sweetly) sickened animus.)

I climb the lime tree,
a zephyr,
neo-classical
and crow carrion.
Their charcoal blackness edifying
and lightly greenish.

*Between the Australian Census of 2011 and 2016's the rate of homelessness in older
women increased by 31% from 5,234 to 6,866 (Australian Bureau of Statistics).

The Unlearned Gesture of Touching Another

after Philip Larkin's 'At Grass'

On cooler days
animals stand closer.

Two mares,
one wears a fringed fly mask, stand together
Pushme-Pullyu style,

an eight-legged, two-headed calm.

The taller lips at the other's withers
as they slowly travel,

this is not moving from,
this is moving with.

The cooler air befits a glamour
of silent sorts.

They quiver,
elevate to sylph
and reactively, gingerly
dance,
echo.

Choreographed on the last cool day,
and now executed without unhinging flies or
a plodding, plotted
atrophy.

It is an ease of closeness,
the unlearned gesture of touching another
is as supplicating
as bathing another in silence.

They part like water
and the mutable thought of it.

Attempting Plush

I attempt
to write about
not writing.

Before the scrape
of pencil on paper
the plush ease
of formulating lines
flows like
a finger's silking swipe,
drips of condensation
on chilled glass,
on contact
the enervating tension
from ear to ear,
the numbness,
dulls the plush
like water
on velvet.

Humboldt's Gift?

The 'gift' hasn't sat for me (as I receive traction and tedium for old injury; crash to the floor 5 years ago, I think of far away things. Not that *Humboldt's Gift* is any way far away, it is a bit uncomfortably glorious. And lifted my poet's heart how and when it seriously needed lifting. Will always credit you with that. The far away things are peripheral to the bearish physiotherapist's force—like your seemingly orbiting, but actually central, 'electron', 'firefly' child-self).

A treasure-like legacy to join, not beat, them?
The purist Humboldt becomes capitalist facilitator/initiator/ conspirator?—I can't 'buy' that, would perhaps call that Humboldt's Joke.

Or the 'gift' is Humboldt's own *gift*—the real deal—rage, high percentage of both dissatisfaction and incarnadine beauty, poetic 'otherness' which society, by its conservative nature, cannot value or return??? Which Charlie Citrine, as wonderful as he is, merely satellites. I understand this to be Delmore Schwartz's gift to Lou Reed, who fully understood. The sand in the machine.

And you?

After Dorothy Porter's Sonnet, 'Is It Not the Thing?'

I do not remember the frisson of his skin,
but I do the sight of his hand;
its fine fingers. His dreamy mouth.
That formal bow of the head;
did he dig in his heels?
I was let go, feral, adept
in ill-fitting, rain-soaked clothes.
(Had just had yum cha for lunch,
my son mishearing a waiter,
'Did he say Profundity?')
If I saw such brush,
situation, illicit heightening
in another
I would razor, ridicule.
Dora Carrington her,
her shotgun's heart purée
to cool, burn us.
Scylla wants to be taken by the hand
and dragged around London Zoo,
stood before Bacon's object depravity.
Wants to braise, offer sex flakery,
Lurex words.
In this time of plague and wreckage
I desire him and bleak parable.
In this time of iris code,
heart stopping cortisol
and back scatter
I desire him and bleak parable.
The raised veins on the back
of my writing hand

are cuttlefished rivers
of flooding pigment and India ink,
are poetry's prismatic eyes,
lodestoned yew, Scylla's wants.
Solicited one letter
with return, unreachable address!
(Oh yes! send another!)
Express, confess, invest! Scintillation;
pure Dot Porter sonnet,
the one about the devil's ice-cold prick.

A Parliament of, with Postscript

Things trickle down through the Internet
as they do. Songbirds nest there.
Such a shame my letters fluttered away
to nothing—why is an unanswered letter
such an unkind, self-made mirror?
Perhaps reflective cannibalism, the Ouse, the Cam,
Slessor's mystic ferry . . . Anyway,
perhaps your reticence helped
my book along—the gulf between Australia
and Therestoftheworld. The one that keeps us
mutually bemused and looking to the desert
for our cyclothymic identity. I wonder
where others look? The book
will come out accordingly—as books do.
Is about my family leaving Hamburg in 1855
and finding Australia a 'good place to get warm'.
My grandfather listened and spoke all day—concentrated
on water supply to the desert and child welfare.
He is remembered as sincere—therefore
not a great success. My 'camp furs of London'
line in his honour—not a pinprick;
a skillet to the forehead.
A bit like cracking a molar
on a roller coaster,
lower right; or paspalum.

P.S.
The unlucky chair-sniffer's encore
was a teary resignation on his way out
of our consciousness, somehow reminiscent

of the evangelism of skincare products
and exercise equipment. Mr Iguana
was caught out playing around
with a young gloater—not as big-league
as Tiger's. Mrs got all Hillary about it—claims
to be a feminist—thus reviving her flagging
career. Last week, since consulting
a stylist, losing his portfolio hence,
Mr Iguana read out a love letter to Mrs
in State Parliament—without the earnestness
of birdsong. A heart wrenching blackbird
outside my window this morning as I tongue
an arabica round my mouth,
some raucous sparrows, wrens,
branch-bowing honeyeaters,
cockatoos dropping small, half-eaten
pears—taxed from where?
My baking dog wary of the windfall
like any lotus-eater,
his belly the colour of blackbird chicks.

Today in Copenhagen
Prince Charlie and Governor Arnie
mash on at the same greenspeak.
Our Kev, fluent in Mandarin and crisp prefect
sips and cheeps, tempered
as unnamed trees, as Patrick White's
car-like, blue Olivetti portable,
its nauseous charioteer.

Guernica 1–4

'A dog starvd at his Masters Gate
Predicts the ruin of the State'

William Blake, 'Auguries of Innocence'

1.

The white dog on the highway
runs like Bede's sparrow,
lifting, golden, through the hall,

like soft thrumming balloons
in a pillowslip,
a dove in milky drift.

It is aware
we pass it,
its turned eye
is Guernica.

Its spilt tongue
the kiss of judges.

Its bullish shoulders
pinked by cars.

Its loose running
incantatory
and ghosted
as I dream
of its exhausting fate,
its legs' winged legs

and their airy perfect
presence
and purchase.

Its Dickensian hustle
and dubious, gracing gate.

The wonder of
its golden sparrow ego;

the otherwise darkness
of the Ven.'s vanishing hall.

No door, or doors,
to claim, hold, keep, rest it.

It would drop
like the ethicist's,
the physicist's,
the Plathian bee.

Growling, howling
another boxed language's
mysticisms and rites.

No other opportunist's
placating windows.

The white dog on the highway
runs like Bede's sparrow,
lifting, golden, through the hall.

Its pace undoes the chrome inevitable,
the brush of abject proximity.

The spinning wheel.

The lost blue ceiling.

The feathers of its tail.

It runs towards
its own thrilling perception of grace.

2.

It runs towards
its own thrilling perception of grace.

The feathers of its tail.

The lost blue ceiling.

The spinning wheel.

Its pace undoes the chrome inevitable,
the brush of abject proximity.

The white dog on the highway
runs like Bede's sparrow,
lifting, golden, through the hall.

No other opportunist's
placating windows.

Growling, howling
another boxed language's
mysticisms and rites.

It would drop
like the ethicist's,
the physicist's,
the Plathian bee.

No door, or doors,
to claim, hold, keep, rest it.

The otherwise darkness
of the Ven.'s vanishing hall;

the wonder of
its golden sparrow ego.

Its Dickensian hustle
and dubious, gracing gate.

Its loose running
incantatory
and ghosted
as I dream
of its exhausting fate,
its legs' winged legs

and their airy perfect
presence
and purchase.

Its bullish shoulders
pinked by cars.

Its spilt tongue
the kiss of judges.

It is aware
we pass it,
its turned eye
is Guernica.

Like soft thrumming balloons
in a pillowslip,
a dove in milky drift,

the white dog on the highway
runs like Bede's sparrow,
lifting, golden, through the hall.

3.
The white dog on the highway
runs like Bede's sparrow,
lifting, golden, through the hall,

it is aware
we pass it,
its turned eye
is Guernica.

Its bullish shoulders
pinked by cars.

Its Dickensian hustle
and dubious, gracing gate,

the otherwise darkness
of the Ven.'s vanishing hall.

It would drop
like the ethicist's,
the physicist's,
the Plathian bee.

No other opportunist's
placating windows.

Its pace undoes the chrome inevitable,
the brush of abject proximity.

The lost blue ceiling.

It runs towards
its own thrilling perception of grace.

The feathers of its tail.

The spinning wheel.

The white dog on the highway
runs like Bede's sparrow,
lifting, golden, through the hall.
Growling, howling
another boxed language's
mysticisms and rites.

No door, or doors,
to claim, hold, keep, rest it.

The wonder of
its golden sparrow ego;

its loose running
incantatory
and ghosted
as I dream
of its exhausting fate,
its legs' winged legs
and their airy perfect
presence
and purchase.

Its spilt tongue
the kiss of judges

like soft thrumming balloons
in a pillowslip,
a dove in milky drift.

4.

It runs towards
its own thrilling perception of grace.

The lost blue ceiling.

Its pace undoes the chrome inevitable,
the brush of abject proximity.

No other opportunist's
placating windows.

It would drop
like the ethicist's,
the physicist's,
the Plathian bee.

The otherwise darkness
of the Ven.'s vanishing hall;
its Dickensian hustle
and dubious, gracing gate.

Its bullish shoulders
pinked by cars.

It is aware
we pass it,
its turned eye
is Guernica.

The white dog on the highway
runs like Bede's sparrow,
lifting, golden, through the hall,

like soft thrumming balloons
in a pillowslip,
a dove in milky drift.

Its spilt tongue
the kiss of judges.

Its loose running
incantatory
and ghosted
as I dream
of its exhausting fate,
its legs' winged legs
and their airy perfect
presence
and purchase;

the wonder of
its golden sparrow ego.

No door, or doors,
to claim, hold, keep, rest it.

Growling, howling
another boxed language's
mysticisms and rites.

The white dog on the highway
runs like Bede's sparrow,
lifting, golden, through the hall.

The spinning wheel.

The feathers of its tail.

Location in the Credits

'lying down in the road and dying
when they could no longer touch each other.'

Judith Beveridge, 'The Caterpillars'

The beauty of his face—
pallid World Cinema.

That wide-eyed immigrant,
that erudite overbite,
that hesitance to speak,
drone for a word.

The slurping seduction
as he stirs the cabbage,
his girl's curls,
intelligentsia's
steaming damp wool,
the Kirlian ringworm
up his sleeves, his breath
catharsis
into the thawing hive
of his hands.

The sting of his disinterest.

The weird (dynamics)
of his beard.
The book he combs it with,
palm-sized
and epic,
read through invocation (his heel),
sung by the angel

on the roof,
its hair burning
like blue butterflies drinking,

electric, then ashen,
London,
then Dresden,
houses,
then fields,
fields,
then forest,
forest,
then bees,
bees,
then ice,
ice,
then desire,
desire,
then disease.

On Your Head, Mr Lear

after 'How Pleasant to Know Mr Lear', by Edward Lear

You,
on your head,
are not remote.

On your head,
you are not misled,
you are not presuming
that the song I sent
was a declaration;
you know it was
pertaining to Bellow.
That its romanticism
was unrelated.
Like Solomon Bellows,
Saul Bellow
and deprecation.
Now, on your head,
mislead, misled, on your
blown egg of a head,
painted for Easter
by puerile, nubile Muscovites.
Frozen butter and bread,
mink, serrated runcible.
Persimmon, scarlet,
crimson, rose
and red.
Birch leaves
like tremulous billboards.
On your head,
Mr Lear—O,
on your head,
Mr Lear.

And what do you wear this Spring, Xipe Totec?
The skin of a sacrifice; yes,
a transcendence of skin . . .
your mouth musing
within his open—O
a tyrannical flamenco provisional.
This deadheaded winter garden
weeps for pleasantries
and pilgrimage
spherical.

O.

Bitterly weeps
for the island's
last crushed plum.

The first discounted simplicity.

Beta vulgaris

'at a desk overlooking
the slum-end of the universe.'

Judith Beveridge, 'The Clerical Angel'

This is not the colour of prudence.
This is Emily Dickinson on steroids,
albeit, at seventeen, a ribbon at her throat like a kitten,
her hair spliced and pegged out by Lilliputians.

This soup mimics filling for a cherry pie.

This is—how can I put it delicately?—that first withdrawal,
that deepest sting, it is—oh dear—Plath's,
of course, haemorrhage.

It is the apologising doctor,
you are a friend of his daughter,
small talk, mons pubis, cervix, a scrape of cells,
you Parvati, stirruped, contemplate the perfection
of his naked feet. You never forget them,
you hear of his death, years later,
repeatedly, in passing; you think of his feet.

It is his wife dyeing her hair in front of you,
she is psyching by numbers,
it lies on a towel across her shoulders
like blue tar on The Empire.
She is India in a small bathroom.

She combs it through, suddenly, seemingly,
aware of you and her need to British you.

'You should wear more apricot', she says. And

'Your mother tells me you used to eat flowers.
They're in the pink of your cheeks.

65

Will you change that light bulb before you leave?

My sister, Deep, is like you, a poet.'

Emily, this is, perhaps, your moon flowered linen, only.

The peeling and slicing of these
colours your hands beautifully.

Their hypercolour persists, their sweetness,
once through you, once tasted.

In this Utopian's slum you eat with awe, a steel spoon.
There is no ordinary Plathian Latin.
You lick the spoon.

You do not write a poem and hide it;
you let it take you by the tongue.

You talk about the first tongue you tasted;
she was Russian, and as indelible
as your nine-year-old self.

You poked out your tongues and tasted.

Her deleted, fisty father drew Europe
with mermaids in the sea,

her brother transgendered,

her mother in a factory, glamorous,
without English, with lips

the high colour of beetroot.

Roth's Sentences

'Everyone picked strawberries, though it was forbidden.'

Joseph Roth, 'Strawberries'

I would share these heart-shaped strawberries, this blood orange
    with Roth.
My thumb finds its rift
like the brass hook and eye of a palm-sized terrestrial globe,
concave hemispheres of the 1756 Northern and Southern skies
within its black pebbled poisson peau casing;
there are monsoons in the Indian Ocean.
We would segment it into lateral gores for Utzen.

The missing child
was known to authorities;
had been treated
for an adult human bite wound
and had attended five days of school
in half a year.

Unseen for three weeks
before being reported missing
five days ago.

She is now being searched for
by divers.

Neighbours hold a candlelight vigil.
She is lost to their everyday.

She is, to my mind, amongst
Roth's delicate, delicious sentences,
his gently thorough rain.

She is amongst the strawberry pickers,
boots off, wading a velvet forest.

His unfinished story ends
thus
[. . .]
as any gritty mouthful.

She is eventually found
in a suitcase
in the ground,
curled like the world.

I Start

Perhaps it came in
with the firewood;

it's not a great leap
from the fireplace to my bed.

A tiny lizard in my hair;
Godzilla in miniature.

Then frozen in the corner
of my pillowcase
like an embroidered alchemy.

It visits a juxtaposition
of cool, silk ferocity.

I start,
I sleep,
regardless
of the freed serpent
caught like a thought
in my hand.

45–47

This self-perpetuating deconstruction
was well underway
when I couldn't
remember,
or
word,
why
it
had begun.

I load firewood into the car without gloves,
but with *echt*,
teardrop pearls.

I talk to a dog I do not know—
he will
not bite.

My heart
burst (again)
as I
felt that
drawing wave
lift and take me,
sieved by treetops,
red plastic gum
tips,
lidded by sky,
fleeced
of everything,

including
failure,
and the oyster's
two-year sadness.
Left only with
things to burn
and lose,
more ways to fail.
Someone's
willful dog.
The car
radio
speaks
of deceit.
A rigged game.

Why do I sigh?

The
dog
plunges
its
nose
into
the back of my knee,
tonguing
for
the
deep,
dark,

sea,
it will perhaps find
a
brackishness.

I send it
from
me
like an eight-legged
magpie.
Its
long
fur
is Evans's platinotype, Sea of Steps, 1903.

Why
do
I
think of
Ginsberg's last poems?

There is still
no compromise
or
disembodiment.

He was never a sublime Bernstein.

Yaka-wow*

There are options.

To learn to play the piano.
To stare at a piano.
To imagine playing a piano.

At this late stage
it is the profound
lack of the profound
that confounds
cognizance,
the burst word-bird,
its loosed springs
like Ethiopian hair,
yaka-wow.

I have decided
you are a cruel slaver,
my love.
My coldest love,
who golden-brains me,
does not care.

You resemble the piano
I imagine playing,
the machine,
the garden,
the swimming elephants, bluish,
delight loop.
The sensory deprivation

of the sensualist
who does not bathe.

*an April 2010 London Times transcription error of British neuroscientist Susan
Greenfield's term, 'yuck and wow', to describe the banality of online reaction.

Till Human Voices Wake Us

after 'The Love Song of J. Alfred Prufrock', by T.S. Eliot

Do I dare/ Disturb the universe?
So how should I presume?
And how should I begin?
Do I dare to eat a peach?
Weldon Kees—at 5am (sounds like a place), buy a recording of Camus
by Camus, The Waste Land and other poems, read by Speaight from
Record and Book Sale in the Blue Mountains. The mountains not
blue. The sky not blue. A tennis court blue. Little boys are coached to
serve. They are told to 'think about it first'.
I do not support the idea of thinking about disturbing, presuming,
beginning, eating. I do support the idea of the peach. Weldon Kees
eating a peach. Frank Harris. Weldon Kees for afters. Just peachy.
A Yaka-wow speech for afters. Imagining playing a piano for afters
(seems it stimulates the brain as much as learning to play). I did not
buy Simple Minds or David Essex or West Side Story. I did sit by the
leaded window in a café.
It did please. Coffee did not. A baby at near table relishing a mashed
banana did. The idea of Camus and Eliot for afters. 'Plurality is all.'
W.K. Think of Prufrock's mermaids' red and brown wreaths for afters.
Where do I get some?
Do I dare disturb the mermaids?
Do I dare become one? A peachy gig.
Idk if they, like Bill Hammond's coastal birds, believe in anything?

Application

We invite applications.
Please do not feel obliged to apply.
You must present with these attributes—
generosity, sincerity, persistence.
Much, most, will be done to relieve you of these.
Their nth will be trivialized, refused.
You must voluntarily doubt, question yourself, continuously.
Your treatment will range from
shabby to dubious to euphoric.
There is the payoff distilled.
Please do not resent the fact.
As you begin, you will not know this;
but you must know this.
We do not recommend soft hearts.
Or crushable heads.
We do not tolerate the unhelmeted ambitious.
Plath refused to wear one.
It suffered. Enough said.
Once the helmet is on, it stays.
Woolf wore it into the river.
Please leave your name, with all its connotations.
You may choose to equate this proffered poverty
with purity.
You may choose to equate it with failure.
You may choose to ignore this.

Nonpareil

His nonpareil non-presence,
disinterest, disassociation
helped to facilitate my absence,
in every sense,
from here.

It digitally shook the hope
from me like a wet bear
– exquisite for a moment;
throwing off crystal arcs.

Then just going through
the motions, the paces,
the cave.

I think I'm trying
to keep it clean,
keep it nice,
until Infrared Nothing
arrives like a loose soul
observed, eyes like
the ocean floor,
wearing fuzz, disquiet,
the powdered dust
of stars,

the unloving world
– it may have noticed
that I have hated it;
it may not.

This camera time-lapses
speeding flowers,
pesters mysteries.

Here comes its sound-bite
of Nothing,
its gritted engineering.

Endearments and Ritual

'Certain mornings, on turning a corner, a delightful dew falls on the heart and then evaporates.'

Albert Camus, 'Return To Tipasa'

A man I barely know,
who I see most days,
whose wife, a nurse,
died driving to work,
her heart just stopped,
passes the café
where I sit each morning,
usually says, hello angel,
asks me what I'm writing,
a love letter?, I say,
a letter to Santa;
this morning he said,
hello centrefold girl,
I laughed like a swaying
Jungian procession, not sure
at what, decided on
his lightness of being,
his existential shopping list,
his ritual tempting of fate,
my (yawning) part. I think,
Do I look like Lucy van Pelt?
This is not my booth;
I am not your therapist.

This Cold-served Anti-poem

Just as the snorer
will not believe,

she cannot imagine
the water
from all those
births—
over two thousand.

Imagine being able to say
William Carlos Williams
delivered me,

knew my mother
before me,

uncoupled us
like two
brown pears,

one inside the other;
or stoned (by his teeth) those/her breakfast plums.

This cadaverous pup
is almost Neolithic,
a fist, deep creases
in a jar,
buoyed like an onion

never knew air.

This tight, soulless egg

this delicious pear

this cold-served anti-poem

The Soul Untied
after Kenneth Slessor

This evening
a rat gingerly executed
the jasmine. And now
fig fetishist
bats chatter
above us,
throw their fell voices
from neighbours' fruit trees,
white-netted like brides.
Black nets—the inevitable;
the hang, the draw, the quarter.
My apple tree un-netted,
ransacked, bitten.
The moon, full and ripe,
drips,
caught in branches.
Meniscoid stars drift loose.
The zoo at night
has come here.
Wings whoop,
slow and solemn,
as we sleepily,
wander, consume,
catch the dark ferry
(eighty kilometres away).
Tomorrow my son is off
picking peaches in the rain.

To Day Squat; the Swans' Resolve

'So much for technique; what about beauty?'

Walter Gropius

The baits in the corners
of the stairwell bring things
that would bite at my shoes
like cold water. I go up the flight
to where I'm falling all day. I lean
over, lower the pail and scoop up
something dark to throw down again.
It makes the sound of a slamming door.
I am downing the flight to where
I'm soaring. It is me kicking through
grass and paper to the station.

This is an old house and
I run through it like the wind.
The rain comes in and wets
the floor like my spilling hands
as they carry water through the house.
It is for the paint smell. I have painted
the carpet with splashes that flicked
from the brush like mistakes
that meander but guide.
My head aches from acetone
and stairwells. Upstairs
I have left things to soak
and ruin, and paint to dry
like burns.
I am deserting nothing
but desertion.

Renaissance

Friends I love like the fine things
they are; one's a Hillary, one's a Lalique,
one's a J. J. Rousseau, one's a Brel, one's
the Bayeux, one's a Wilde and one's a tribal
Warhol. (Others are animated tribe.) They have
left and are leaving me. Oh my. Me oh. My heart
it runs after them. Before them. With them. It
clenches on departure. It waves through windows.
It wavers through and over bodies and faces. It
wishes well. It has a talent for attachment to finery;
it loves. We share the cling; keep the faith. (Sweep
zee air wiz zee 'arnd!) That is direction.
Return the empties. This is rhetoric. This is narration.
Fill them. Return them full. This is my renaissance.
There are my friends.

When I Said, He Never Wood, I Meant It

Touching van Gogh's chair; he was not a leg-man.
This is the asylum chair. On/In this
he would have sat and wept and despaired.
Wrote letters to his brother; mon dieu, mon cher.
Theo! When the trees were bare in Summer.

So I touch the seat and get him where he lives.
It is on the ceiling. I sniff my fingers
for man or child; but they smell of art
and Sien. (Here we differ. She holds her child
like a stranger. They are the Mother and Child
of 1883; it is skeletal. It is wooden.)

That same day I got a letter from a
French translator. He translated my name
into poetry. And I suffer in the translation.

Theo! When the trees are bare in Summer.

Ticket

The return half of a train ticket
jammed into the spine
of the first poetry book
I bought
got there five years ago
like a fisherman's knife
opening an oyster-shell
to find a pearl
to put on my tongue
and swallow slowly
like a fifteen-year-old
swallows patience.

It separates two pages
of Michael Longley's 'In Memoriam' poem
like a child does parents;

I remember putting it there, and
I remember loving that poem
as much as I loathed the pearl.

Domain

Speakers in the park
speak from boxes
and experience
piled high in the dark;

stepping on people's fingers
and intelligence.

Acknowledgements

Thanks to David Musgrave; valued ed. Ross Gillett; the people of P&W—thanks to the warm, young and immoderate crowd at Sappho's, on the cold night of the 9th of May, 2017, who first heard 'The Munchian O' vocalized, lifted from Aleppo and 'the page'—especially Lindy Morrison, Tricia Dearborn and Pam Brown; thanks to Greg McLaren and Toby Fitch—abiding thanks to Adam Aitken, Judith Beveridge, Stuart Cooke, Helen Garner, John Hawke and Martin Langford—love and gratitude.

'A Peacock Sweeping' was first posted on the online journal *Plumwood Mountain: An Australian Journal of Ecopoetry and Ecopoetics*, volume 4, number 1, February, 2017.

'Better Boy, Early Girl and Green Zebra', first published in *Yellowfield* #11, April, 2016.

'Rewild' on Plumwood Mountain, volume 3, number 2, August, 2016, 'Rewilding' in *Contemporary Australian Feminist Poetry*, Hunter Publishers, 2016, 'The Apes Sang' in *Zarf*, issue 3, February, 2016, 'The Film Student's Shoes' on Cordite Poetry Review 50.0: No Theme, May, 2015, 'World's End and Gadigal' on Cordite Poetry Review 47.0: Collaboration, August, 2014.

'Response to John Hawke's Poem, 'The Demolition of Hotel Australia' (reading Patti Smith in a Hailstorm)' and '*Beta vulgaris*', *Plumwood Mountain*, volume 5, number 1, February 2018.

'Germaine's Postcard' was first published in *Blue Dog*, volume 2, number 3, 2003, 'To Day Squat; The Swans' Resolve', *Rubicon*, number 8, 1987, 'Renaissance', in Another Site To Be Mined, *Poetry Australia*, number 107/108, 1986, 'When I said, He Never Wood, I Meant It', Young Poets' Issue, *Poetry Australia*, number 103, 1986, 'Ticket', in New Pressings, *Poetry*

Australia, number 96, 1984 and 'Domain' in *Poetry Australia*, number 81, 1982.

'The Munchian O' poem was longlisted in The Ron Pretty Poetry Prize 2016 and won the 2017 Gwen Harwood Poetry Prize, published in *Island*, 151, 2017.

An earlier version of this manuscript was shortlisted for The Helen Anne Bell Poetry Bequest Award 2017.

Notes

'The Munchian O'

'The poetic transfiguration of childhood carried out by the bourgeois nineteenth century is so much stuff : there is nothing poetic about a child whatsoever. But it is true that for a child the world possesses a fascinating strangeness—always providing that he is lucky enough to be able to gaze upon it and explore it.'
de Beauvoir, S. (1977) *All Said and Done*, Penguin Books, London, U.K.

'If Life Has a Base That It Stands Upon'
Dearest Creature's letter is from page 204 of Washington, P. (ed.) (1996) *Love Letters*, Alfred A. Knopf, Inc, New York, U.S.A., Darling Mongoose's is from page 179 of Glendinning, V. (2006) *Leonard Woolf: A Life*, Simon and Schuster, London, U.K., some sedimentary pieces are from page 46 of 'The Mark on the Wall', from Woolf, V. (Woolf, L. ed. 1944) (1991) *A Haunted House—and other short stories*, Grafton Books, London, U.K. and 'A Sketch of the Past' and 'Old Bloomsbury' from Woolf, V. (1985) *Moments of Being—a collection of autobiographical writing*, A Harvest Book, Harcourt, Inc., New York, U.S.A. provide the poem's memoir.

Meredith Wattison, born 1963, a poet and essayist, her six books of poetry are *Psyche's Circus* (Poetry Australia, 1989), *Judith's Do* (Penguin Australia, 1996), *Fishwife* (Five Islands Press, 2001), *The Nihilist Line* (Five Islands Press, 2003), *Basket of Sunlight* (Puncher & Wattmann, 2007) and *terra bravura* (Puncher & Wattmann, 2015), shortlisted for the 2016 Kenneth Slessor Poetry Prize.